DIRECT DIALLING

DIRECT DIALLING
Carol Rumens

CHATTO & WINDUS · THE HOGARTH PRESS
LONDON

Published in 1985 by
Chatto & Windus · The Hogarth Press
40 William IV Street, London WC2N 4DF

British Library Cataloguing in Publication Data

Rumens, Carol
   Direct dialling.
   I. Title
   821'.914   PR6068.U6

   ISBN 0-7011-2911-5

Copyright © Carol Rumens 1985

Photoset by Rowland Phototypesetting Ltd
Bury St Edmunds, Suffolk

Printed in Great Britain by
Redwood Burn Ltd
Trowbridge, Wilts

ТЕБЕ

Contents

Acknowledgements & Notes

Acknowledgements are due to the editors of the following magazines, in which some of these poems have been previously published: *Ambit*; *The Honest Ulsterman*; *Poetry Book Society Supplement* (1983); *Poetry Review*; *Thames Poetry*; *The Times Literary Supplement*.
Acknowledgement is also made to Faber and Faber Ltd and Random House Inc. for permission to quote from *The Collected Poems* of W. H. Auden, edited by Edward Mendelson.

'Zvezda' – star (Russian).
'Sixteen Dancers' – the poem is narrated by an imaginary woman, a chess-player. The 'sixteen dancers' are the sixteen chess pieces.
'Revolutionary Women' – Nechayev was one of the early Russian revolutionaries seeking to overthrow the Tsar.
'Winter' – the Burlaki were the towing-men of the Volga River.
'Escape From White' – 'inostrantsa' means 'foreigner'; 'pravda' means 'truth'.

I would like to thank the Arts Council of Great Britain, the School of Continuing Education at the University of Kent, and Dorothy Goldman, in particular, for her encouragement.

DIRECT DIALLING

A Prague Dusk, August 21st 1983

'About a subjugated plain,
Among its desperate and slain,
The Ogre stalks with hands on hips,
While drivel gushes from his lips'.

W. H. AUDEN

I

When his broad shoulders turn
in their leaf-coloured uniform
and square up to a doorway
on Revolucni Street,
he might be any soldier
and the bar, any girl,
its response no more than a certain
heightened inattention.
He orders beer and seems
as innocent as his thirst,
straining his young white throat
to greet the last drop,
but the great, mellow, cultured
pearl of Mitteleuropa
has dimmed behind him;
shadows slide unchecked
from the medallioned buildings
scaffolded up to the waist,
numb veterans who have learned
how short the life of honour.
He smiles, provincial, brash,
half-tame. The careful hands
that have served his purposes
slink off and busy themselves
with rows of glasses, small
change. Eyes follow him out,
each glint of hate a coin
with its own private value.

2

That he could not master speech
no longer seems important.
Perhaps only a poet
word-trafficking in the free-
market economy
of Oxford or New York
would have thought it a fatal weakness.
One blast of his breath was enough
to seal the twelve bridges.
With a few phrase-book phrases
he is armed for years to surprise
and amuse the populace,
his weight sunk deep in its silence.
Impassioned flattery
on the cut of his Westerner jeans
is not expected when,
naked as his fists,
he strides down Vaclavski Namesti
with his shuffling train of echoes:
what happens, happens without us.
We forget only the present.
It is the pall of memory
that sticks like morphine to the nerves
of the empty August city.

3

Going home on the metro
the children chatter
but the mother is almost asleep.
Some sweet, unscripted dream
is drifting across her face,
follows the droop of her arm
to the grasses that nod in her lap.
It's already dark
on the staircase where she hushes
and stumbles; light from outside

shines on the two pairs of shoes
placed at each nuptial doorway,
intimate and exhausted,
moored like little boats
in an ocean of drudgery.
When she too, at last,
is sitting in stockinged feet
and the children asleep,
she will recall each detail
of the picnic: how the country
they walked through never changed,
monotonous and tender
as the afternoons of motherhood;
how tall the grass became
when they lay down to rest
and the stalks rose silvery miles
and whispered to the sky.

A Soviet Army Tenor

The Russian voice, it's said,
has risen a whole tone since the nineteen-hundreds,

pushed up by nervous insincerities,
but the song that flickers high off the cassette

was earthed before the censor's chalk screamed
on the clean slate, or irony bit its lip.

And the choir, gathering leisurely reinforcements,
is only a windswept platoon of firs,

a chained sigh, an unhonoured
show of strength in the field of robbed time.

Medals burn in the studio-lights. But listen
to the soft, irregular, excited breathing

of the only animal said to have a soul.
He can silence his own kind

in multiples, blindly obeying his hands,
yet, when the mood takes him,

he remembers his disproven soul, and wishes
that every army could become a choir,

and the battleships dip their turrets
in shame at having borne the names of men.

Zvezda

Our new bright candle-light lists on its stem
as if you brushed it with a secret question
and the flame sobs a little and rights itself.
We cannot be unguarded yet. We stop
and start. Ash crumples into the glass star.
Words are the shaken salt of memory.

Just then you saw your childhood glimmer up
to be swept away in the hands of the Chinese waitress.
People came from the East, from beyond the mountains.
They kept the markets; they were brisk and kind.
One day they simply vanished. Snowflakes massed
outside your grandmother's window; that was north

where childish questions freeze. But yours came back,
the faint cries drifting nearer in your head
with each year's pencilled inch. Pure dissidence
– clean as a severed artery; the swift
plunge of a dying hand; the mixed reds
pouring and fading on the steel of exile.

There are no wolves, our only lies are white ones
in Camden Town. The anxious candle eats
them slowly, yet the tellable resists us.
I could argue that democracy can cheat –
but my past is a doll's house no-one kicked,
yours, a tower of malevolent offices

without doors or stairway, its vague windows
blinking through the black sleep of empire.
Pictures of impossibility: a wife,
children, parents, childhood; so much
stolen in order to build the better world,
and what wasn't stolen, you gave.

History withdraws, leaving the bill
that would choke this candle in its cradle-dream
tactfully face-down. Stretch your hand
over the table, whisper to me in the language
that always sounds so sleepy and wants to be kissed.
Then everything will blur into a fable

we'll improvise together, about a star
(a red one or a white, it makes no difference).
Dreaming of five continents, it fell
one day from the flag on which it was emblazoned
to become an ash-tray, to become the word
you teach me, frosty, bright, untouchable.

Outside Oswiecim

1

Let me tell you the story of days, handsomely printed
in dawn and darkness, in sleep
and in burnt-eyed longing for sleep.

2

It puzzles the secular light, this polyphony
of dim cries. I wasn't there, I heard nothing,
yet the air is so full of them, I could sing them all.

3

When the train banged to a stop and whispered 'where?',
then they began. Some rose, some fell. The sky
rushed in like sea, we opened our mouths, it drank us.

4

It is hard to lose everything, harder to despair.
Those words on the gate, some dreamed of them, and loved
to walk in their shade, suck out the iron of their promise.

5

In the night, the bright light; in the wire, the stopped heart;
in the eye, fear; in the crust, hunger;
in the rock, uranium; in the world, Oswiecim.

6

Dumb narrative curiosity keeps you from the wire
how many times? You watch yourself, amazed,
whipped to a panting run past outstretched arms.

7

Death's clever, he has maths and capital,
but life's a tough nut, a phlegmy knot,
and nearly chokes him, like his Prussian collar.

8

They wanted us corpses and they wanted us
grave-diggers, they wanted us music, machines, textiles.
They kicked us as we fell. How human they were.

9

It was Erev Shabbat, evil was fallible.
A shaved girl smiled in the sun. An angel had murmured
'Amen' before he saw the gesturing dead.

10

And what if his Lord had heard that some of them
were raging animals, and still sent day-break, still
sent no-one to stroke them with their names?

11

No, no, the question is obsolete.
Nothing sees nothing. Mercy was down to us.
Our mouths jammed shut on nothing.

12

Emblem, exhibit, witness – Husserl's suitcase
flanked the rust-brown pile. The cold twine of its handle
I touch, then grasp for a faceless, weightless stanza.

. 13

Child, enchanted at gun-point, whose child are you?
Come here, take off your cap, don't cry.
How is it possible I can make no difference?

14

Oh they crowd in, death's kindergarten. Small grazes
scared them once. Their eyes are always yours.
I'd take their pain, here, where your absence is.

15

I loved in you, yes, what made you strangest.
The desert gave you its shadows. I'd watch for ever
the poise of your smile, its bland, half-mocking stillness.

16

Another race is only an other, strolling
on the far side of our skin, badged with his weather.
In love or hate we cast looks, hooks; get it wrong.

17

How shall I bear your indifference without hate?
It stirs in the dust, a length of hose. If I burn
how shall I not flex my whip near your eyes?

18

No, come away, put on that riddled cloth
of the centuries, be ash and stone, your stare
like his, a star.

19

They beckoned, they turned their limbs this way and that,
they whispered, you tried to get near enough to hear,
but the heat roared at you – take your eyes and run.

20

Not 'the six million', not 'the holocaust',
not words that mass-produce, but names. One name;
Husserl's, perhaps. His favourite food, his new watch.

21

Where death's made now, you must wear protective clothing
Yes, we are still perfecting the science of last things.
Our blaze will be the best yet. Will you drink to it?

22

Chosen to illustrate the idiot's tale;
An illumination from the Book of Fire,
Sand and Next Year; chosen to be most mortal,

Our pyramid swam and sank through the nitrogen
Fog as starving crystals ate our air.
Christ, to whom the soldier said 'Go on,

Call down your god if he's got ears and brains',
You would have understood our short-breathed terror.
Poor rebel son, you also wore our chains
In dumb commitment to the tribal error.

So we died for the last unforgeable scrap
– Ourselves. Got free for being something harder
Even than zoo-meat. Fought like the Crusader
To nail our resurrection to the map.

Northern Woods

Small enterprises line the exit roads
out of London . . . then the bankruptcies . . .
and the long haunting of her absence begins
in a delirium whitened by birch-trees.
They sidle past, existentialist poseurs,
with a soft slippery shine that is barely a shine
– what light is there in the world for them to borrow?
Go on, they say, dissolve into drugs and tears;
we are her trees, we are your memories
blank with all she could not bear to tell you.
But I never cry. I just keep driving, staring.
When I left her for the last time, our hopes
the sea-smashed continent, my flight-bag heavy
as a new tongue, I learned to swallow fire.
Now the colourless bottle leaves me sober
as a vision of birch-woods, growing colder
and cloudier as they get to Pietarsaari.

Sixteen Dancers

1

One night in our first week of marriage
you asked me to meet you in your favourite square.
It's easy, you said. I was to look for the postcard
you'd sent me once in Prague.
I remembered the small, feminine fountains,
how I had stared into their silvery weather
and tried to taste the sea.
Now my feet crunched pigeon-food, gravel, wet ice.
And there was the lion you'd climbed, jeans slithering
on the cold bronze, ten years ago, to shout
for Ho Chi Minh. You were late. Traffic snarled
in circles; I waited at the centre.
How small it was, after all, this famous square.
I looked down at my coat, my shoes, my handbag.
Gifts. Yours. London's. Not mine.
And then that English snow I'd refused to believe in
came feathering into the wind, little iron tongues
licking my face. My shoulders had turned to salt
as I stared east, towards home.

2

The tournament hall was like school,
with tables, and a ticklish, whispering silence.
I wasn't scared, I always did well at school.
I decided not to look at my opponent.
He was bigger than me, and we both knew he'd lose.
Parents, opponents, boyfriends, the state
– I laughed at all of them, I was never scared.
My mother dragged my hair back, plaiting it
cruelly, tugging my brains into three.
I snipped the plait off whole,
and pegged it on the kitchen line; she screamed.
I revelled in such private enterprise,

the thrust of Machiavellian knights and cut-throat
bishops; power flickering like black magic
from palace to proletariat and back.
It was a picture-book I'd never tire of,
and each new story always began the same:
once upon a time there were two great kings.
One lived in the east, and one the west.
And they were enemies though they were brothers.
Each knew the other king like his own face.

3

Some heads had been guillotined from the family album.
No-one seemed to know why.
Poor faceless ones, I searched for evidence
of wickedness in watch-chains
or the grey folds of skirts where wrists lay broken.
At last their wounded innocence burned through,
silencing my childish accusations,
like the starry cherry-flowers on Namesti Miru.
They murmured: The Russians are here!
I was fifteen. It was thrilling, like the first taste
of melon each year, or plunging into the water
at Marienbad. The walls burst into posters,
the wind chased leaflets, hands flew everywhere.
The soldiers lounged and smiled like elder brothers.
Then the holiday was over,
the grown-ups silent as suitcases.
Our leader bowed his head, got into the Chaika.
The chairs stood back, as one by one,
my friends, no longer thirsty, left the singing.
They were like the people in the photograph
changing colour as I lay the page
on wood first, then my hand.
I sulked. My mother cried. My face grew thin.
I moved my wooden men to win, to win.

4

When they teach you your past is a lie,
they extinguish your future.
When the party-machine drives words into your mouth,
starvation becomes acute.
When friends disappear, the door of your heart bursts open
merely to reveal another door.
When the spotless spring parade shines on the trees,
you blink, and brush the petals from your eyes.

5

You were the reigning British Champion,
your suit like a blue coffin, your hair like leaves.
Beneath the fire-weeping chandelier,
sat Timman, neatly torturing Polugayevsky.
The hall was emptying. I'd won my game.
Yours was adjourned. A small crowd had gathered
at the smell of blood.
We stood together, held our breath and watched.
In the silence I felt your concentration lapse.
You touched my arm, and we walked softly out,
linking smiles in a world of foregone conclusions.

6

You courted me smartly, eloquent, careerist,
but perfect-mannered, versatile at checkpoints,
customs, hotel-desks. Our sweet receptions
bloomed among the low-line teak veneer
like an elaborate, creamy, high rococo,
tumbled out of nowhere, out of time.
And this, like time, was always quite beyond us
– a liberty we took, and couldn't take,
the morning after, homing to our boards
and clocks, the slow, meticulous invasions;
nationality seeping back, the silver cups
spreading their wings, the draped flags, the speeches,
the return-ticket, and the correct papers.

7

Architects, accountants, friends from Oxford,
arrived at eight in the flat you called the cupboard,
and I, the manor.
Your eyes challenged them with a lovely fire,
as if you'd risked your neck to bring me here.
(The builders had only just left,
taking the earthquakes and the thunder-storms
but leaving the rainbows, as you had commanded.)
The flat was floured and trembling like a geisha.
Your friends pushed everywhere,
coughing a little, spilling drinks, at home.
One, I remember, spoke Czech:
and I, on my third vodka, told the joke
with the ice-and-lemon punch-line: what are the Russian
troops doing in Prague? They are looking
for those who invited them.

8

Sticky Fingers, Soldier Blue, Rough Trade:
I walk, take taxis, walk. My carrier-bags
multiply. It rains. The pavements darken,
the dust smells antique. My feet get wet.
I don't care, my shoes have turned to knives
in spite of hours of choice and wads of plastic.
I'm in the wrong element. As for marriage,
it cost me a country. Once, I queued
all day for a chrome teapot, dumb with hope.
I never dreamed of flight as now I dream
– in samizdat, my thoughts fluttering
always towards my murderer, my accomplice,
whose fingers check me, who looks up and smiles.

9

You know how it is with us.
Living out of suitcases, we fly
from game to game, from story to story,

new faces on the loose change in our pockets.
You know how lonely it is
— the faint taste of a different language,
and the hotels, always the same yet not quite,
and the smiles at the opening dinner, the same, but not . . .
and nothing ever quite real.
You know what it is to win,
and how the rules change then,
or how we think the rules change then.

10

Marriage as an inventory:
mine, the Bohemia crystal;
yours, the Chinese rug;
mine, the silver fox,
the dolls, the rosewood box
of marbles, the kitchenware, its brave colours.
Yours, most of the books,
and all but one of the war-games.
Mine, the thirst;
yours, the cup.
Mine, the fault;
yours, the freedom from guilt.
Mine, the manor, ruined.
Yours, the cupboard, empty.

11

The radio, left till last
because we can't decide,
squats on the floor and mutters to itself.
We would orphan it if we could.
Instead, we try and listen to its news.
Someone should be making tea;
someone should be quietly crying.
But everywhere it talks about is far away.
There is no mention of our fallen city.

12

Postcards telling jokes or lies
– I could write home on any of them,
send them from nowhere, never to arrive.
The stones of Prague, the sharpness of your eyes
I shall never see clearly again.
Ten years on, what do I know about you?
That you have a wife. Her name.
That her star is Virgo and she is virtuous.
That she has fair hair and is fully-armed.
And what do you know about me?
That my victories are few. That I defect
regularly from those dictatorships
my lovers make of passion. That I claim
more freedom than there is in any world,
except the world of men.
Still, I'd go down your winter streets again
to break a glass for one last toast. Bright-lipped
with sweet liqueur, we'd kiss and drink to life
– the life no kisses ever made less bitter.

13

How impassively they face each other,
the fighting men, before the players arrive.
A woman in overalls hoovers round the tables
indulgently. The fighting men exchange
the wan smiles of platoons on Christmas morning,
remembering cigarettes and oranges,
and what they still have left of being human.
The woman slides her hoover
noisily into the passage.
Dust twinkles in a sun-shaft, breakfast smells
seep from the kitchens. It is quiet, domestic.
The fighting men seem to have chosen peace
before the players arrive.

14

One eye on the clock, one ear on silence,
we take our sixteen paths into the darkness.
Outside, the universe of moves is flowering.
We have some choice. It dwindles. Who or what
chooses how we chose need not be asked.
It is enough to see that acreage
shine at our feet: first, the unharvested
squares of sun and shade; later, what's left
in the democracy of broken hopes:
– this we call freedom, I and my sixteen dancers.

Blockade

Europe has been broken:
a panacea of banks,
steel cladding, the black
fugue of Berlin.

Oh Linden Tree, oh Linden
I cannot breathe
without your small hands, your great shade.

Aubade

Light as a rose
he sleeps beside
his first cradle,

intent on stillness
but breathing firmly
as if breath would always

give itself back.
He has travelled far
to be in his flesh,

to learn what happens
and to forget.
His existential

smile is perfect.
It tells me how
he will offer himself

when the time comes.
But for now he will keep
his excellent secrets

– the glossy function
of heart and lungs,
arms and legs,

the legend of his mouth.
His voice sleeps,
his sex sleeps.

In the faint shine
of morning when
flesh can be chilled,

I draw up the sheet
and cover him
to save us both.

Circe

Now we are nothing. It is as you wished
when we last held each other.
I saw you boyish, crass, forgivable
and mythic with departure
– but it was something that you'd come at all.
Surely your presence under-wrote return
and surely all the brightness in your eyes
belied the casual phrase
by which you cut adrift our misty future.

Oh yes, I had your warm life by the neck,
yet somehow washed you in oblivion
like Lethe, for you went from my bed
that afternoon forgetting everything.
What is between us now? No conversation
or kindness – merely waves
that roll pig-grey, rinsing the silent cables.
Each night I try and drink my way across
– a moth-like weaving
to find the chancy formula, the voice.
Sometimes I drag it to the telephone.
My finger slips, I've been too long alone.
I could do an aria or a speech
perhaps, but how make small-talk of so much?

I think of you in sunlight
your body dark, local drugs on your lips,
god of the vines, banal as an advert
but for the greedy shining in your gaze.
It falls upon Penelope, betrayed
that afternoon, so unimportantly;
you take her now because she's there, and simple,
unspoilt as the little cove you've found.
She has no song but offers you her mouth.

You give her all your kisses,
nicknames, money, whims (she loves you child-like
among the brilliant in the best hotels).

The breeze at sun-fall flares
suddenly and shakes your salt-stuck hair.
The fig-trees start their soft, accustomed screaming.
Our northern dusk is slower,
a schmaltzy, dim, blue church for sick abeyance,
with love and pleasure always somewhere else
– Eden, Jerusalem, Arcadia.
The sirens can be moral – if you care.
Remember me, my faithful touch, my shape
before I aged, became entirely graceless,
all envy, all desire, all lack of hope,
condemned to sail upon a self-wept sea
each year-long night, Odysseus, of your absence.

Vocation

Is it poetry I'm after at those moments when
I must clothe your hands in mine or comfort your shoulders
– so bare and neglected sometimes when we wake –
or press your mouth to taste its uncurling flower?
Is that which seems so fleshly and truthful merely
a twisted track into words, a way to leave you
for your image? Art is tempting, a colourful
infidelity with the self, and doubly feigning
when what is repossessed secretly by one
was made by two. And I wish I could pour a poetry-vodka
into twin glasses we'd gulp unanimously
('I poison myself for your health' the appropriate toast)
but only a poet would have acquired the taste
for such a strange distillation; you'd never warm
to heavy-petting dactyls, the squeak and creak
from locked, suburban stanzas. And so my fingers,
dancing alone, are less than content. They perceive
how they have clung to moral adolescence.
Their vocation now could be simply to talk to your skin,
to take you at kissing-time; later, to close your eyes
by stroking the lashes lightly over cheekbones
flushed with some high, bright, childish fever, and so
write the poem in the touch-shapes of darkness
and let it end there . . . They are on the tip of trusting
this silent, greyish room, its astonishing view
fading from metaphor to the life with you.

In the Cloud of Unknowing

Goodbye, bright creature.
I would have had you
somewhere on solid earth,
wings clipped to pale

shoulder-blades,
and your fleecy head
a chrysanthemum, darkly
grown from my pillow.

I would have kept my tongue
for what salt weepings
it could tease from your finest
silences.

But it was written
into your book of life
that I should be brief.
Forbidden to count

the ways, denied
et cetera,
I worshipped the stone
from your supper-time plum ,

the little hairs gleaned
in tears from the sheet.
Metaphysical desire
was all they would bear,

a bandage of art
for the low sob
of the vernacular,
a condition of prayer.

Now when I wake
and the dawn light names
your perfect absence,
I am at home,

lapped again
in my earliest language,
the vocatives tense
with desire and distance:

'Thou who art called
the Paraclete';
'After this our exile';
'Oh Sacred Heart!'

Dear iconoclast
forgive these texts
their cloudy haloes.
The intent pen burns

its slow path through
the slant rain of Greek,
the stars of Hebrew
. . . to touch your hem?

No, it was never
possible.
The old mystics knew
as they closed the book

on the dancing colours,
worn out with words
never made flesh
and with flesh that fought

their long abstraction.
They listened a moment;
the breath-soft foot-step
in the cloisters faded

as always to sighs;
the cold congress of leaves
in darkening autumn;
the wind's dissolution.

Pavane for the Lost Children

When you rest in my arms and your heart
quietens against mine
I think of a midnight kitchen,
the kettle muttering on the lowest gas,
and the baby forgetting to feed,
lips plumped like a little mollusc
that is almost losing its grip.
They could not relinquish survival,
those lips; I knew what they dreamed of
would keep arousing them
to fits of greedy, absent-minded tugging.
So I sat on, enthralled,
and my breasts wept ceaselessly
like the fated wedding-jars.
This too is our grown-up devotion
when fatigue is most pressing:
to pretend we will never put each other down
and drift singly away on
sleep's disappointing persuasions;
such lowly forms of life, so deeply marine,
we cannot move apart, or know what time is,
but are turned like bivalves on the lifting wave
that has promised us to the sand.

Time Trouble

I know all about these German wrist-watches.
They try to wake you with tinny, insect-like tunes
by Kapellmeister Beethoven,
as the digits flip over on your bedside table
and my old-fashioned minute-hand
flies to your neck and whispers nervously
with that little pad of fat where your head is thrown back
because you're still in an ecstasy of sleep,
and your suitcase not yet packed.

Once upon a time
they'd take me to admire the German clock
in the museum. There were wooden figures inside it:
Jesus at wooden supper
with his twelve wooden apostles.
And when it struck three, they said,
the apostles filed out
and all bowed woodenly to Jesus
except Judas, who swung round the wrong way.

I never stayed to see this remarkable dumb-show.
By a minute to three, I was going to be sick;
I turned my back on the clock, the crowd
fell apart with a hiss.
As I race down the shadowless aisles,
though the horrible whirring has not yet begun,
I can see it all perfectly
– mad Jesus, his nodding guests,
and Judas, the simple materialist,
turning on his clockwork,
showing us his chalk-white face.

Revolutionary Women

Nechayev, dreaming of Tsar-death,
wrote about three categories of women,
and how they could be harnessed to the cause.
The first he dismissed as painted, empty.
You could twist them, break them, toss them away.
The second were good comrades, passionate
idealists, willing workers,
but dangerous finally, and disappointing
– their values weren't political at all:
they too must be discarded or reformed.
The third kind were the true revolutionaries;
deft with gun-oil, bullets, high explosive.
They'd take a lover only for his secrets,
milk him fast and leave him in his blood.

I know I'm with the second sort, cherishing
nothing better than a just cause,
except perhaps the man who'd die for it;
who grows entranced, watching allegiance crumble
and rebuild itself in curious gothic snow
like candles at the hovering hour of sleep.
Turning soup into a bowl I've started
at a white face in the china, both yours,
Nechayev, and that of any bourgeois
gazing up in naked appetite.
This is what causes the strong hand to falter.
Armies, official and unofficial, learn
that what they kill aren't men, or are only men.
But we, that regiment of the starry-eyed
you need and fear and try to educate,
who type your manifestoes through the night,
may still in the morning be discovered,
the counter-revolution breathing gently
beside us on the pillow, while the Tsar

goes to breakfast, and his men to torture.
In our loose night-gowns warm and obvious,
too slippery to cement a single brick
of the just state, even the state of marriage
– Nechayev, you'd be right to gun us down.

Winter

It begins in secret
with mist, a dazed bee
in the lavender-bushes
and radiators mild
as human skin.
This would be May
to your serious habitat,
the iron-black river
that is its heart-line,
wobbly as a frontier,
untrammelling itself
in endless dissatisfaction.
I think of the Burlaki
trussed in rope
like performing bears,
who trudged the plashing weight
of their servitude
to the rhythm of the thaw.
You bow your head,
fists on the table,
chest-notes swelling,
and silence the room
with their empire of grievance.
In your perilous climate
the wind has already fastened
stiff white grave-clothes
on the auburn water.
It settles everything
like the hand of a lover.
So the winter river
accepts its birth-right
calmly, as you must
– the massive silences,
the gift of utter cold –

locked in its own
solid crystal, surveyed
by a few tethered craft
hungry for a new trade
of skins and revolution.

Escape from White

'Here, people's eyes, like the cities of this country
Are large and clear; never does the soul's tumult
Move the pupil with an extraordinary glance;
Never does desolation cloud them over long.'
    ADAM MICKIEWICZ, 'Forefathers' Eve'

Slowly the bruise of afternoon lavender deepens
to bilberry, and slowly it seems to withdraw
from my approach, the sea-coloured coastline of sleep.
An edge of chalky moon appears, gets cloud-lost;
the book in my hand thins to another window.
Where in this walled city shall I go, where shall I turn
in the almost-white June night, and evade my need of you?

The cathedral swims like a whisper out of the sweat
of coppery lights. What nerve it takes to retrace
our descent into heavenly ordinariness when we roamed,
camera-hung tourists, hand-in-hand through St Stephen's
on a mid-summer morning quiet as ourselves;
when, moved by your extraordinary glances,
I saw you admire the parochial, upright, lawn-trimming,
France-hating, surly soul of this dreariest county.

I was busy observing you with my old affection
for the edges of maps, that breath of the East you bring,
irresistible as the anecdotes once told me
by the milliner's girl, my Kentish grandmother,
whose hair as she swanned by the Medway glistened so
    black
the sailors sang at her "Japalady!" If only
you'd naturalise me to your strangeness, I too might gaze
on this cabbage-patch with tender, sea-grey eyes.

Idiomatic now, you perfect your tongue
with irony and bad grammar. Who would guess
from your study of gardens, supermarkets, cars

and American-English, that your true pursuit
is a moral example; how, in secret anguish,
you whisper to the child that dares not hear you
"But look how well this other one tries to behave!
Why can't you do the same?" And you almost pray
for the end of that damaged life, abandoned now
to the crocodile technicians of survival.

Each day abroad takes you curiously closer
to the narrow, silent, intimate hospital-bed
where the flesh is kept alive but whitely blank,
and you stare into eyes that cannot sleep or see,
their last wild doubt fixed in a glaze of sedation,
until the lavender dusk, the cathedral and my hands
with their foolish island behaviour of grasping and closing,
fade into the sombre night of your pilgrimage.

From the moment of touch-down you were free to fly,
and, at the first embrace of an *inostrantsa*,
to enter the terrible candour of homesickness.
Sometimes its waves swell to such a height,
I fear for your life; sometimes I think your heart breaks
whenever I say your name. If love exists,
is there more love in it than truth in *pravda*?
What can it do but take from you this gift
of night and bear the mourning it permits?

A Jewish Cemetery

1

At dawn they are one great shadow, whispering.
They are warning their children:
don't break the backs of your books.
Sunset. The shadow multiplies;
the backs break.

2

Among the swaying sighs
and the candlestubs, gothic with catarrh,
wanders the upright citizen. He is bored
and uneasy. He shoves the broken bits
of alphabet with his illiterate boot.
What else, these days, can you do with the past?

3

The closed books.
East looks West and sees East.
West looks East and sees West.
The apocalypse rides both ways.

4

Names must often be silences
in this city, in this world.
His block of flats is dark
and hollow like a chimney.
I climb it twice a day,
doubling my heart-beat
as I touch the bell that bears
his faded, biblical name.
My hope spirals up
and falls back, levelling
with my lack of hope,
a conversation of kinds
between the flame and the ash,
between the name and its silence
in this city, in this world.

Direct Dialling

To trade in bliss
alone would never
be permitted us;
I understood this
from the start, although,
girlish enough,
I bought the dress,
and fed the scene
to my moment-adoring
Polaroid;
a little window
of flower-dotted green
that trembled in
your attentive hand.

But our faces, sad,
already told us
of time and the state
– their thirsty methods:
the prisoner reading,
heart-in-mouth,
a thumb-stained letter
three winters old;
his wife bringing
his yearly half-hour,
like a wound they must both
stroke to bleeding.
Our kindlier pain
is simply this
rinsed teapot packed
in a cardboard box
with your cook's knives.

Where the law can't reach
mischance has set
his ancient looms;
he doesn't forget.

We faced across
the empty table;
could no more touch
than if watched. You,
silently smoking,
re-read the airmail,
its soldierly lines
of refusal shaky,
barbed like wire.
'What can I say
to your invitation?
Do you suggest
I betray my country?'
Then, later on,
'All my friends are dying.
I'm old and alone.'

Letters, 'phone-calls
— those vanishing sparks
in the great places
of absence and
fidelity;
the summer nights
ringed by ice.
Prometheus,
you wake each day
in your distant city,
stung in the ribs
by the acid spear
of prison-food;

and when you sleep
it's a kind of flight,
desperate, intense,
and, you say, dreamless.

We stand in line
to snatch a moment.
Our conversations,
furtive, hoarse,
hang by a thread
at midnight. Where
could we build our house,
by what dispensation
secure the loose sands,
the iron winds –
and our sturdy, late,
bilingual child
scatter, regather
the brightened stones
of all your loves?